Wildlife Wong

and the

Pygmy Elephant

by
Dr Sarah Pye

Wildlife Wong and the Pygmy Elephant
September 2021

ISBN: 978-0-6451543-2-0 (paperback)
ISBN: 978-0-6451543-3-7 (ebook)

Published by:

estralita
PUBLISHING

Estralita Publishing
ABN: 86 230 144 690
P.O. Box 288
Buddina, QLD, 4575
⊕ www.sarahrpye.com

Pencil sketch illustrator: *Ali Beck*
Cover design: *Gram Telen*
Layout design: *Gram Telen*
Wildlife Wong cartoon illustrator: *Isuru Pltawala*
Cover author photo: *Amber Grant*

A catalogue record for this
work is available from the
NATIONAL LIBRARY OF AUSTRALIA
National Library of Australia

Check out what other kids think about this book...

"Wildlife Wong and the Elephant is an educational book (but not boring) that's easy and fun to read. It explains the bigger words to kids who may not understand them and includes cool experiments. I have learned some really interesting facts about elephants!"

Zoe, age 13

"I especially enjoyed reading this book, as the elephant is my favourite animal. The facts are extremely interesting and I have learnt so many new facts about them. I really am glad that there are people like Wildlife Wong looking out for the elephants and helping to protect them. The experiments look fun and I can't wait to try them out!"

Joe, age 10

"This book is very entertaining and unique. I liked how I was able to learn new words like pygmy and dung. The book is very fascinating. I think that kids and adults would love to read this book."

Lakeesha, age 10

Wong and Sarah in the rainforest

Hi! My name is Sarah. I wrote this book about my friend Wong. He lives on the island of Borneo which is the world's third largest island. Do you know what the *largest* island in the world is? If you said 'Australia' it's a really good answer because it *is* an island. But Australia is defined as a **continent**, not an island. A continent is the name given to a really large area of land. The other continents are Europe, Asia, North America, South America, Africa, and Antarctica. Which continent do you live on?

Check out this map of Australia and Borneo!

The largest island in the world is Greenland. It's a strange name because most of Greenland is covered with ice. The island of Borneo, on the other hand, is VERY green, VERY hot and VERY humid. The rainforest in Borneo is home to more than 200 different mammals. Do you remember what a mammal is? (We learnt about that in *Wildlife Wong and the Sun Bear*). There are also 400 different types of birds, 100 different **amphibians**, (which means a cold-blooded animal which lives in water and on land), and about 400 species of fish. Borneo sounds crowded, doesn't it?

This book is different

This book includes a story about Wong, lots of cool facts and interesting activities so you can pretend you are a scientist just like my friend Wong. It is the third book in the series but don't worry if you haven't read the other books yet. You don't have to read them in order.

When you have finished, perhaps you would like to make your own book? If you go to my website, www.sarahrpye.com, you can join the **Wildlife Wong Kids' Club**. There you can find videos of the experiments, download pages for your own **Nature Journal** and a template for making a **unique** cover (which means one-of-a-kind). Does that sound like fun? I'll remind you again at the end!

Want to make your own book?

What's this book about?

The first two books in this series are about Wildlife Wong and two different mammals that live in the rainforest – the sun bear, and the orangutan. THIS is the third book. It is about his adventures with the LARGEST mammal in the rainforest – the pygmy elephant.

What a funny name!

Pygmy means something very small, but the pygmy elephant is the largest mammal in Borneo. What a strange name!

Have you ever heard of something called an **oxymoron**? No, it's not a rude name you call someone you don't like. An oxymoron is a saying where two words are put together that seem to be opposites or **contradict** each other. 'Small crowd' is an oxymoron because a crowd means big, not small. 'Old news' is an oxymoron because OLD and NEW are opposites. Do you think 'pygmy elephant' is an oxymoron?

Even though elephants are so big, the species got its name because it is the smallest elephant in the world. But when Wong was being chased by one, it didn't seem very small!

Tracking bears

When Wildlife Wong first arrived in the rainforest, he wasn't looking for elephants at all. He was looking for sun bears. He wanted to track and trap them so he could take measurements and learn important things like *how* they lived, *where* they lived and *what* they ate.

Being a scientist is sometimes really difficult. Wong trampled through the forest for three years on a bear hunt and he only managed to trap six bears. Can you imagine that? It's the same as one bear every six months, or 182 days! Luckily, there were so many things to do and learn in the rainforest that he didn't get bored. And Wong didn't get too lonely because he had two people helping him — Guy and Chia-Chien.

Check out
how high
sun bears
can climb!

How do you trap wildlife?

Trapping wildlife doesn't always mean catching animals. First, Wong wanted to spy on animals without them changing their behaviour, so he decided to use a **camera trap.**

Sometimes when you walk into a shop, the doors open automatically. They do that because they have a **sensor**, pointing towards you. When it **senses** movement, the device opens the door. A camera trap works the same way except it sets off the camera shutter to take a photograph and *traps* an image without hurting the animal.

Just after sunrise, Wong loaded his backpack with a heavy metal box, a large camera, sensor, battery pack, a roll of photographic film, a metal bar the shape of a T, a map, compass, a box of last night's left-over noodles and a huge bottle of drinking water. He hoisted the bag onto his shoulders and clipped the straps across his chest and waist. Then he reached for his lucky hat, plonked it on his head, pushed his glasses up his nose and started walking into the forest with his **machete** (a cross between a knife and a sword) in his hand.

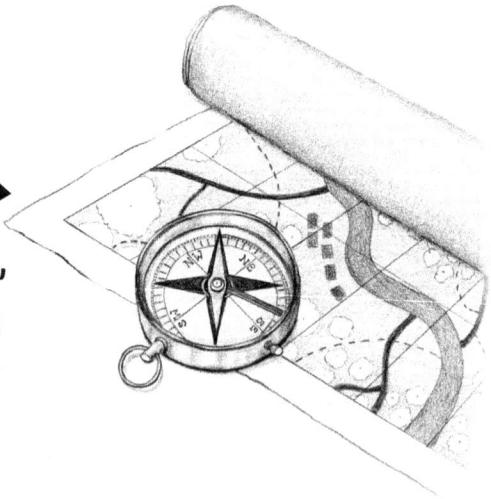

Do you know how to read a map?

As the buildings and people disappeared behind him, Wong's eyes and ears became **attuned to**, or aware of, the forest. He scanned the leaf litter below his heavy walking boots for signs of sun bear poo. He searched for **decimated** (or destroyed) logs where sun bears had eaten termites. He circled huge dipterocarp (dip-tero-carp) trees looking for claw marks, and he squinted into his binoculars looking for honeybee hollows high in the branches. He would set his camera trap wherever he found **evidence** of sun bears.

The deeper Wong walked into the forest, the **denser** the undergrowth became, and the slower his progress. Pill millipedes rolled up into tight ping-pong-sized balls to protect themselves as he passed. Barbet birds sent warning calls to each other to keep away. But there was no sign of sun bears.

Pill millipedes
have amazing
armour

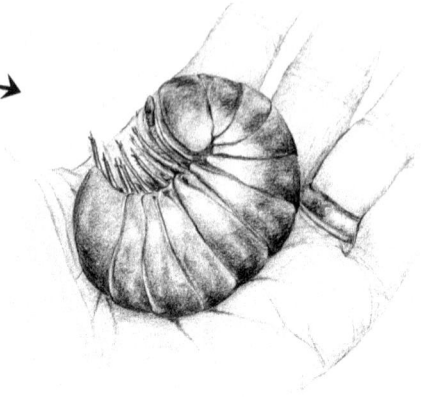

As Wong slashed through the forest with his machete, he grew hot, tired and hungry. He wished there was a path to follow. As if by magic, a gap appeared in the undergrowth. The plants had been flattened into a path about as wide as a city path or sidewalk. This would save time! Wong unrolled his map, consulted his compass and estimated the spot on his map. He then continued **cautiously** because paths like this one are only made by one type of animal… an elephant!

Not far along the path, Wong found a pile of poo. It wasn't sun bear poo, as he had hoped, but elephant poo, or **dung**. He stopped to look or **observe**. It looked like horse **manure** (which is another word for poo), with large, rounded clumps. He sniffed. Any bad smell had gone. A mushroom grew out of one of the smaller clumps. Rain had **eroded** the dung so he could see grassy **fibres** and next to the dung he could just make out the remains of an elephant footprint.

All these signs told him the elephants were long gone. Wong breathed a sigh of relief and continued on. Hopefully, he wouldn't come face-to-face with an elephant.

Around the next bend, Wong smiled. The tree before him was bright orange where its bark had been torn off. He investigated further and found claw marks leading up the tree trunk. This was the place for his camera trap!

Setting up the trap

Wong sat down on a log and emptied his backpack. His lunch smelt good, but he resisted eating until his work was done. He opened the film canister and took out the film **cartridge**.

I am guessing you haven't seen old-fashioned photographic film? Well, before mobile phones had cameras, you used to have to buy a roll of film in a cartridge. It was a strip of plastic covered with chemicals which reacted to light, and it would only hold 36 images. When the camera shutter opened and shut very quickly, the light burnt an image into the film, and the film moved forward to the next **frame**. This picture was called a **negative** because the colours were reversed. The lightest areas of the image appeared dark, and the darkest areas appeared light. The film was **developed** in a photo laboratory which stopped the colours changing. Then the negative was projected onto special paper to make a photograph with the colours the right way round.

In the forest, Wong **shielded** the camera from direct light with his body, opened the back and fed the end of the film into the winder. He closed the camera, checked the connections between the camera and the sensor, then packed everything into the metal box. He attached the metal T-bar to the box and lifted it to chest height against a small tree (about as high as a sun bear standing up) with the camera lens pointed towards the claw marks on the bigger tree.

Wong leant on the box to hold it in position as he screwed the T-bar into the tree trunk. He would return next week to see if his camera had 'trapped' any images of sun bears! Now it was time for lunch!

Photography can be dangerous

A week later, Wong drove along the logging road until he was close to the point on the map where he had placed the camera trap. This time his backpack contained a spare battery for the camera, and another roll of film. He planned to change the film and battery then return to the car.

This is fresh
elephant dung

PHOTOGRAPH: © BENOIT GOOSSENS

Wong moved quickly through the forest with his compass and map in his hand, but there was something different about the rainforest this time. He could smell elephants. He slowed his pace. Fresh elephant tracks disappeared around the corner. A pile of dung lay on the path, steamy and smelly.

There was another smell too. It smelt like sweaty socks and rotten cheese mixed with skunk spray. It reminded Wong of when he worked in a goat farm. (That's a story for another day!) When he used to get home from the goat farm he used to go straight into the shower with his clothes on because he smelt so bad! Wong knew the elephant smell was more dangerous than the goat smell. When an adult male elephant was in **musth** (which sounds like 'must'), it excreted a smelly liquid above its eye, and it was sometimes very angry.

Wong spun around, scanning the rainforest. You would think elephants would be easy to find, but they are amazingly good at hiding. He couldn't see anything unusual through the trees, so he continued slowly towards the camera trap.

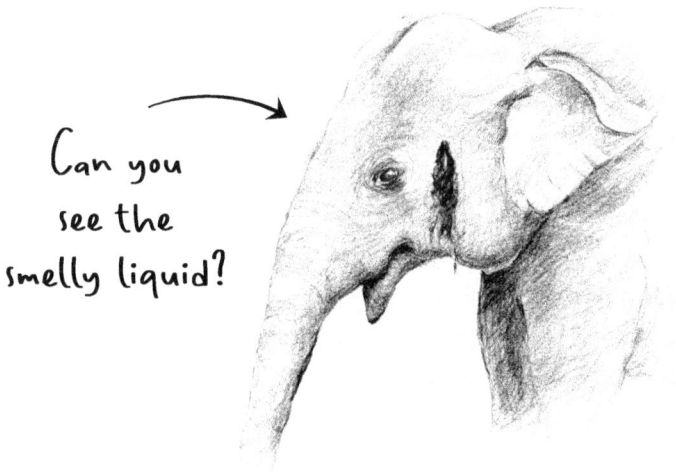

Can you
see the
smelly liquid?

When Wildlife Wong reached the spot on his map, the camera was gone. Oh no! Wong searched for his precious equipment. It was important for his research, and very expensive. Finally, he found the metal box fifty metres from the tree. Thankfully, the camera was still inside, undamaged.

The nasty smell was still strong, so Wong worked as quickly as he could. He levered open the watertight box then checked the tiny number on the camera. It told him all thirty-six photos had been taken. Sometimes this was because leaves or branches had caused the sensor to go off, or **misfire**. He wouldn't know until the photographs were developed. Wong was nervous as he took the next step. If he didn't wind the film all the way back before opening the cover, valuable negative images would be gone forever.

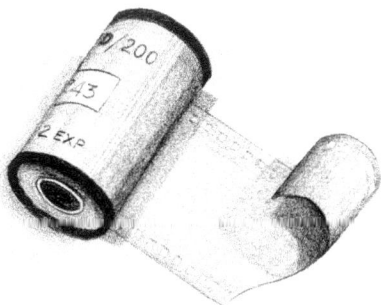

He carefully removed the roll of film and placed it in an empty plastic film canister. He then inserted a fresh roll, packed the camera back in the metal box, attached the metal T-bar, and screwed it onto the tree. Wong turned and made his way back to the car as quickly as he could.

Portrait of an elephant

While Wong waited for the **technician** to process his photographs, time moved as slowly as the classroom clock on the last day of school. Eventually he was handed an envelope. Inside were 36 photographs. He couldn't wait until he got home to look, so Wong opened it right there. The first one showed a common Malay civet slinking through the forest at dusk. The next was an out-of-focus **macaque** (a type of monkey which sounds like 'ma-cak') swinging on a vine. The third was an un-recognisable grey shape in the dark. As he flipped through the rest of the stack of photos, the grey shape came closer, and closer, and closer. He could make out the shape of an elephant's trunk. Then a large grey ear. Then a blur. Then an upside-down eye. Then three upside-down toes. There were plenty of portraits of elephants but not a sun bear in sight! Better luck next time…

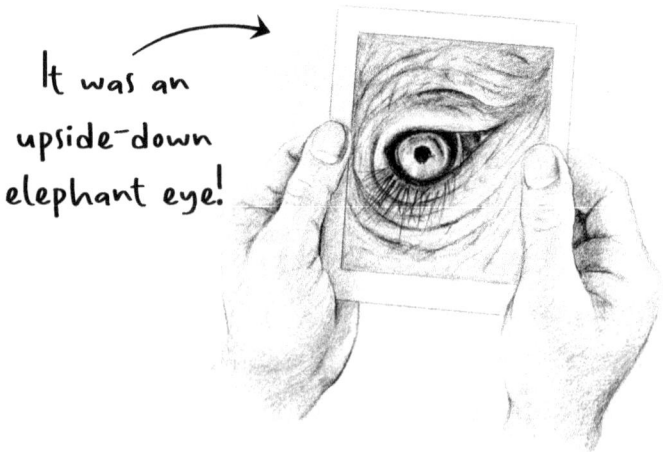

It was an upside-down elephant eye!

A lucky escape

Elephants live in families just like humans do. Their families include sisters, mothers, grandmothers, daughters and sons. As the sons grow up, they create a teenage gang, and when they are adults, they often leave the family and go in search of their own family. These **solitary** male elephants are the most dangerous and Wong needed to avoid them.

He decided to stop tracking bears on the ground when elephants were sighted in his study area. It was safer to use his car instead. "If we were in the car, we could outrun an elephant, but on foot it is difficult!" Wong said.

It was a good plan… but it didn't always work.

This male was pretty scary!

One day, as Guy and Wong drove along the logging road, a group of teenage elephants blocked the road. This is sometimes called a **bachelor** group. Wong slowed the car to a stop and waited for the elephants to move away, but the elephants were naughty. They wouldn't let Wong drive through. The biggest teenager **pivoted** towards them, (or turned on the spot) with his ears flapping wildly to scare them off. He had large tusks and Wong could see the stain from a trail of watery liquid running down the side of his face. This told Wong the elephant was in musth. Wong twisted in his seat and looked over his shoulder as he backed the car away slowly, but it wasn't enough. The elephant started charging.

"Go faster!" yelled Guy! Wong pushed his foot down hard on the accelerator. He weaved his way along the narrow road as fast as he could in reverse, with the elephant kicking up the dust in his tracks. Just as he was wondering if the elephant would catch them, it stopped, turned, and swaggered away.

"Phew," said Guy, "That was close!"

Tracking with a radio collar

Wong **persisted**, and one day, the photos from the camera traps came back with pictures of sun bears! He was really excited. Together, Wong and Guy strapped pieces of his aluminium barrel trap to their backpacks and carried them into the forest. When all nine pieces were in place, they assembled them and baited the trap with chicken guts to attract sun bears.

After a few days, it worked!

Wong and Chia Chien **anesthetised** the bear (gave it medicine to make it sleep) then fitted it with a radio collar and set it free. Now they could track the bear using the signal from the collar! It was much safer.

Wong and Chia-Chien with the first captured bear

The best place to track the bears' signal was at the top of the fire tower. This tall wooden structure was like a massive climbing frame in the forest, taller than the trees, with a platform near the top. Wong wanted to track the bears non-stop for one 24-hour day each week. Guy stayed at the top of the tower during the day, and Wong was there through the night. They only had one car, so Wong drove Guy out to the tower early in the morning. Then, as the afternoon shadows were as long as they could go, he again drove out with Chia-Chien, their camping equipment, and food. Chia-Chien set up their picnic dinner at the top of the tower, while Wong drove Guy back home.

It is always wet in the rainforest but one day it rained especially hard. Wong drove back up the steep slope to the fire tower slowly, looking forward to his dinner, but his car got stuck in thick mud. He tried to reverse but the car wouldn't move. Wong waited a moment then tried again but the car sunk deeper. Luckily, it had stopped raining and he didn't have far to go, so he unpacked the equipment and walked the last stretch with his arms full.

Tracking bears from the fire tower

It was almost dark when Wong climbed the tower, and the deafening sound of cicadas moved like waves through the trees. He greeted Chia-Chien then lit the hurricane lantern and hung it above their picnic. In the distance, they could hear the trumpeting of elephants.

As soon as Wong and Chia-Chien put down their chopsticks, the elephant herd crashed through the jungle below. They didn't sound happy. Wong reassured Chia-Chien the tower and platform were solid, they were in no danger, but dark always makes things a little scarier. The sound of twigs breaking and elephants munching sounded much louder in the dark.

Wong's car looked like an elephant had sat on it!

At dawn, the **pachyderm** visitors were long gone. Wong and Chia-Chien packed their things and made their way down the steps. As they walked through the forest to the car, they looked around nervously. The sight that greeted them was shocking. Wong's car was no longer stuck in the mud. It was several metres further down the road and it looked like it had been in an accident. The windshield was pushed in and cracked. The right side was dented like an elephant had sat on it, and the bull-bar hung like a wobbly milk tooth. They pried the doors open and brushed **shards** of glass from the front seats. Wong held his breath as he turned the key. Thank goodness, the car started. They drove slowly back into camp.

Elephants and humans

The leader of an elephant herd is the oldest, wisest female. She is called a **matriarch** and she knows where to find food. It is not in the deepest part of the forest, but in clearings where the trees have been logged, and on the edges of the forest where the sunlight **penetrates.** She leads her family from food source to food source and Wong learnt that she chooses a predictable pattern, moving on often to give the grass and foliage time to grow back.

Juicy grass grows at the river's edge

One of the best places for elephants to find food is along the banks of the Kinabatangan River (Kina-bat-ang-gan) where thick, delicious grass meets tasty water. This muddy brown river is the second longest river in Malaysia. Besides elephants, it is home to proboscis monkeys with big round noses and fat bellies, screeching families of pigtail macaques who scamper up tree trunks, gliding saltwater crocodiles who use **stealth** to sneak up on their prey, prehistoric pangolins with their armour coats, camouflaged clouded leopards, and long-armed gibbons whose booming call can be heard three kilometres away. And that's just the animals!

Which bird do you think this is?

The birds along the river include darting kingfishers with pointed beaks longer than their heads, purple herons with necks in the shape of an 's', and pied hornbills which look like they have a second beak on top of their head!

People also live along the river, and tourists like to visit. The first time I visited Kinabatangan River with my daughter Amber, she was 11 years old. The pink sunset was reflected in the water as we climbed into a wooden longboat and sped across the water.

It was dark by the time we reached the wooden cabin where we would spend the next two nights. As we unpacked our bags, we could hear an elephant trumpeting in the forest behind the cabin! We ran quickly back to the boat and the captain took us up and down the river hoping to see them. They had disappeared.

Kinabatangan River is important to wildlife

Hundreds of elephants **migrated** up and down the river in search of food. Sometimes they walked 45 kilometres a day. The government decided humans and wildlife needed to share the river so they made a law that all farms must be at least 150m from the river's edge. This created a safe **wildlife corridor** just for animals. It was a very good idea, but sometimes a farmer planted his crop 150m away from the river and, over a year or two, the river moved closer, and the corridor disappeared. Then elephants were forced to walk onto roads and into farms. Sometimes elephants broke things, or ate a farmer's crop.

Can you imagine what it would be like if an elephant crossed the road in front of you? What would happen if you were driving too fast? What would you do if an elephant walked through your garden and sat on your gate?

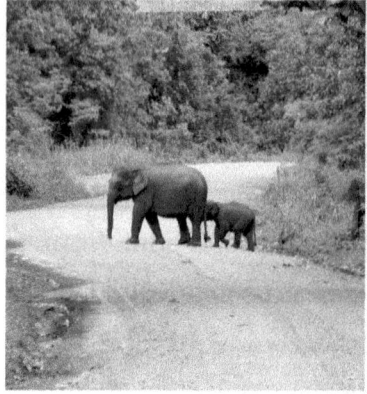

I hope you aren't driving too fast!

Lost and alone

One day, Wildlife Wong needed to go to town for groceries. He left his rainforest research area and drove along the logging road. Ferns grew thick right up to the edge of the road and he knew many animals loved the juicy new leaves. Sometimes they came out of the bushes in front of his car, so he drove slowly.

Just as he expected, up ahead the leaves to the right of the car rustled. Instead of the common bearded pig or long-tailed macaque, a small, dark grey, hairy pygmy elephant poked its head from the bushes.

Wong slowed his silver truck to a stop and the calf **sauntered** up to his car, sniffing it with her **dexterous**, or skilful, trunk. Wong opened his window and turned in his seat to watch. Her long tail, which almost touched the ground, disappeared behind the vehicle. He turned to his left, just as the baby reached the back door on the other side. "Where is your mother?" he asked her in the Malay language. Wong didn't want to get caught between a mother elephant and her baby. If there is one thing more dangerous than a teenage elephant, it is a mother in protection mode.

"Where is your mother?" Wong asked her

Wong moved the car forwards slowly, but the young elephant followed behind. He went a little faster, but she still followed. Wong stopped the car about 100m from the baby and she ran towards him just as if she was following her mum. Maybe she thought the silver car was her mother.

Have you ever found an animal that needed your help? Was it alone or injured? What did you do?

Wildlife experts suggest the most important thing is making sure YOU don't get hurt too. So, Wong didn't get out of the car. He knew the calf's mother could appear at any moment. He also knew that sometimes a herd would **abandon** a calf if she smelt like humans, so he didn't reach out and give her a pat either. Neither did he give her food and drink because he knew that could make the stressed baby sick.

Wong used his phone to take a GPS reading, which is the same as recording his position on a map. Then he called the Sabah Wildlife Department and told them where to find the lonely calf. His job was done. It was really hard for Wong to drive away and leave the poor little elephant alone, but he knew help was on the way. Do you know the phone number to call if you find an injured animal?

The Sabah Wildlife Elephant Team arrived in their big truck. They found the calf not far from where Wong said she was. First, they investigated the whole area to see if they could find the baby's mum, or herd, and reunite them. Unfortunately, they couldn't, and they feared her mother had been killed by poachers.

They **coaxed** her onto the truck and made sure she was comfortable. Then they drove her to Sepilok where she was given a huge bottle of special elephant formula. Before long she had made friends with the other rescued elephants.

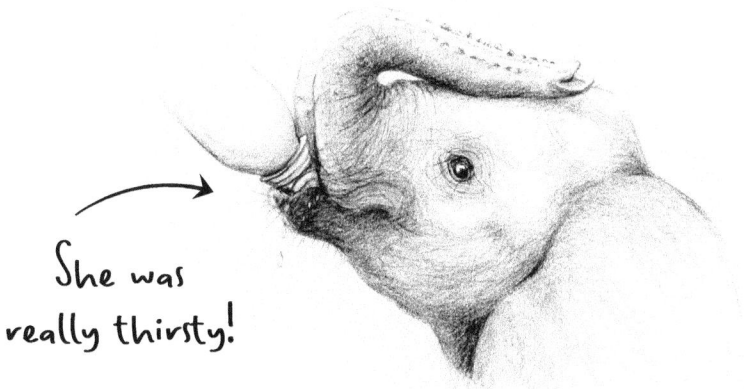

She was really thirsty!

This all happened a long time ago. The calf would be all grown up now. Wong now works at the Bornean Sun Bear Conservation Centre in Sepilok. It is right next to the elephant rescue enclosure. When I visited him, I walked past the elephant enclosure on the way to the bear house. I wondered if one of the grown-up elephants inside was the baby Wong helped rescue. Secretly, I hoped she was not there. Perhaps she was able to re-join her herd and is **roaming** free back where she belongs. I imagine her as the matriarch of her own herd. Or maybe, just maybe, she even has a calf of her own.

Want to know more about pygmy elephants?

Did you enjoy that story? Now, why don't we learn a little more about pygmy elephants. Perhaps you can use this information for a school project! After that, it is time for you to become a scientist!

The smallest elephant in the world

Elephants are the largest living land mammal on earth. There are basically two types of elephants — the African elephant and the Asian elephant. These are divided into six different species and the Bornean pygmy elephant is the smallest of all. The largest elephants in Africa are sometimes 4 metres tall. Pygmy elephants only reach about 1.5 metres. They weigh less too… African bush elephants can weigh 6,000 kilograms. that's the same as four small cars. Pygmy elephants weigh about 3,000 kilograms. How many small cars is that?

African Elephants

Asian Elephants

African Bush Elephant

Indian Elephant

Borneo Pygmy Elephant

African Forest Elephant

Sri Lankan Elephant

Sumatran Elephant

Why are pygmy elephants different?

A very long time ago, (about 420 million years ago) most of the land of Earth was joined together into a land mass called **Gondwana**. In the **Jurassic** period (200 million years ago) when the dinosaurs were around, this land mass began to break apart. Over millions of years, sea-level rose and fell as the climate got warmer and colder, changing the shape of the pieces. Our continents are still changing today, and so is our climate.

About two million years ago, Borneo was attached to the rest of Asia in a land mass called **Sundaland**, and elephants roamed wherever they wanted. Then, about 300 thousand years ago Borneo broke away from the mainland. The elephants in Borneo stayed in Borneo, and the ones in the rest of Asia stayed there. Over time, the elephants in Borneo **adapted** to living on the edges of the rainforest. They became smaller, grew longer tails, straighter tusks and developed larger ears than their Asian cousins.

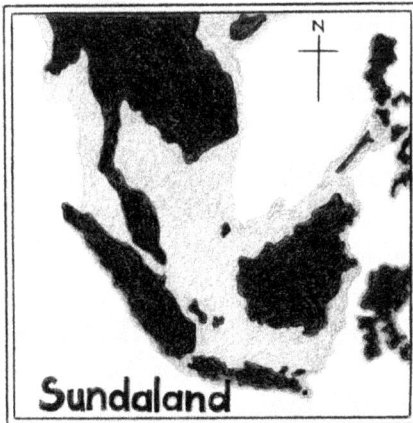

Sundaland was a huge land mass

Parts of an elephant

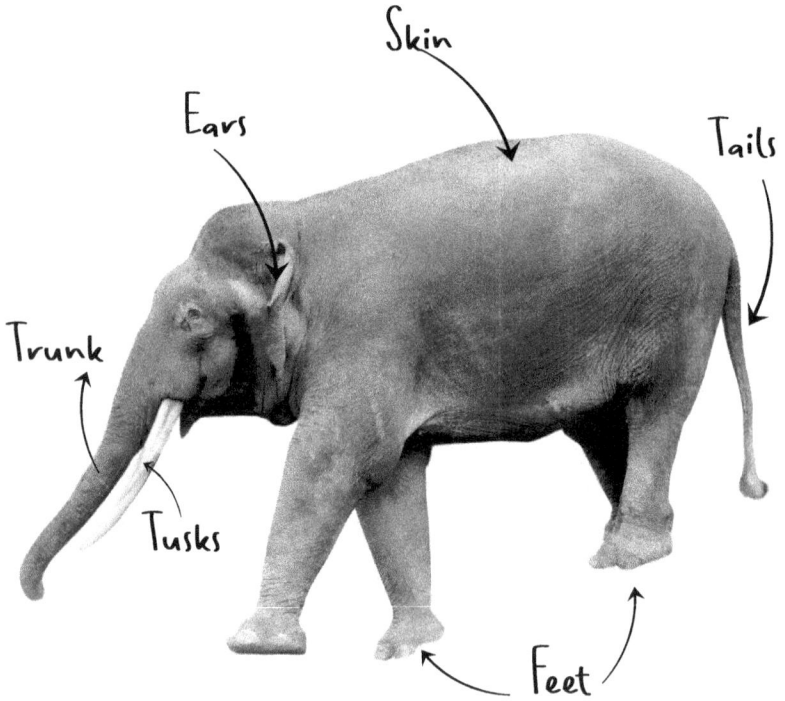

Skin

Ears

Tails

Trunk

Tusks

Feet

All elephants have grey wrinkly **skin**. Their skin is really thick, especially on their back and head. Sometimes when they roll in the mud or dirt, they look brown, orange or black.

All elephants have trunks. The **trunk** is the elephant's nose and upper lip together. There are no bones in the trunk but there are about 150 thousand muscles! Elephants use their trunks for all kinds of things like washing, making noises and saying hello. When elephants greet each other, they wrap their trunks together. They love to bathe in the river and suck up water in their trunk to spray each other. The trunk is also useful for making a trumpeting sound when they are excited or angry. Can you make a sound by pushing air down your nose?

Some elephants have **tusks**, or really long teeth, which extend from their upper jaw. In Africa, both male and female elephants have tusks, but in Asia only male elephants have them. African tusks are curved like bananas, but in Borneo elephant tusks are straighter.

Tusks are used for digging, gathering food and fighting.

African elephants have larger ears than Asian elephants. Elephants' **ears** act as air conditioners. They contain thousands of blood vessels close to the skin. When they are hot, elephants flap their ears to cool their blood. Flapping their ears also makes elephants look more **menacing**, or scary, as Wong discovered.

All elephants have **tails**, but Bornean pygmy elephant tails are sometimes so long they touch the ground.

Elephants make rumbling sounds to communicate which we can't hear. The rumblings travel through the ground to other elephants who listen to the vibrations with their **feet**!

How long do elephants live?

Humans are the longest living land mammal, but elephants are not far behind us. They can live between 60-70 years in the wild.

What do they eat?

Elephants are herbivores, which means they only eat vegetation, not meat. Pygmy elephants eat grass, fruit, palms and banana plants. They only sleep a few hours each day because they have to spend most of the day eating.

Can elephants remember everything?

Have you heard that elephants have really good memories? Well, it's true! A pygmy elephant's brain is 3-4 times larger than a human brain. Scientists have found that pygmy elephants never forget a face. They can keep track of 30 different individuals in a herd and recognise themselves in a mirror.

When
Jenny and
Shirley met

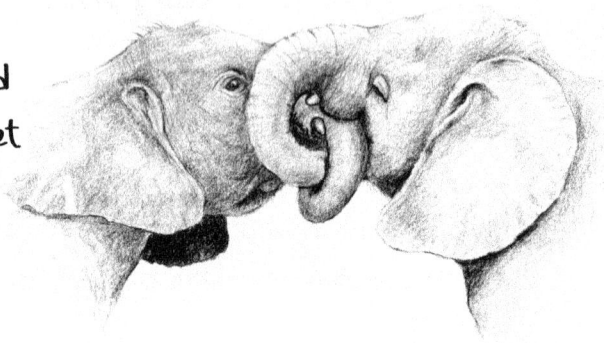

One zookeeper called Carol Buckley noticed an Asian elephant called Jenny was really excited when a new elephant called Shirley came to the zoo. The two appeared to know each other. Zoos keep records of their animals, so she went back to the office to read their history. Carol found Jenny and Shirley had both been in the same circus 23 years before!

Why are pygmy elephants endangered?

Bornean elephants are at risk of extinction. They are listed as endangered because there are only about 1,500 left in the wild. The numbers of elephants are **decreasing** (going down), but the number of humans is **increasing** (going up). Humans need homes, roads, and food and often this means there is less habitat for wildlife. When bad things happen between wild animals and humans it is called **animal/ human conflict**.

One day, the Malaysian government decided to build a bridge between two towns near the Kinabatangan River. It would make life much easier for people, but much harder for elephants. Many **conservationists,** including Wildlife Wong, were angry about the plan. They wrote letters to politicians to voice their opinions.

After nine years of protesting, the plan to build a bridge was dropped. Wong and his friends were very relieved. The elephants could continue migrating along the river without added danger. "This is my country. I grew up here," Wong said. "I must protect my own country, and my own wildlife."

Elephants
need a
home too!

PHOTOGRAPH: © MACARENA GONZALEZ

Have you ever written to a politician about something you feel strongly about?

If not, maybe you should!

Experiment 1

Casting footprints

Scientists like Wong spend time **in the field** doing their research. This doesn't mean they are hanging out at the farm. It means they are in the environment conducting their research. When Wong is in the field, he is in the rainforest observing evidence of animals. Evidence helps him learn how animals live. Can you remember what sort of things he found in the story?

Let's hunt for evidence of animal footprints near your home, or school, and make a cast to take home!

You will need:

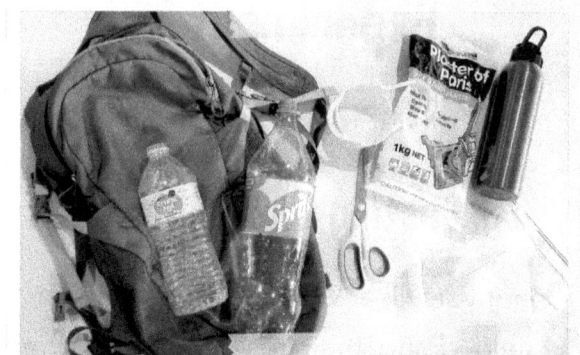

A large plastic bottle

A small plastic bottle

Scissors

A backpack or bag containing:

- Water in a bottle with a lid (about 1 litre should do!)
- A bag of Plaster of Paris powder. (You can get this from a hardware store for under $10)
- A measuring cup

- An aluminium cooking container or old plastic takeaway container for mixing
- A stick for stirring. You can use a lolly stick, or any stick you find while you are hunting
- Two sealable bags for taking your casts home
- Another bag for your rubbish

Steps

(Check out the video at **www.sarahrpye.com**)

Getting prepared

1. Cut the plastic bottles into rings about 3cm wide. These will be used to put around your footprint. It is good to have two different size bottles for different size prints!
2. Put all your equipment in a backpack.

Searching for footprints

Let's go!

1. Choose a place you think you will find footprints. I like going to the beach, or along a trail through the forest, but you may be able to find prints in your garden or a park too!

2. When you find a well-defined footprint, place a plastic ring around it and gently push it halfway into the ground.

Making the cast

Now you need to mix your Plaster of Paris so you can make a cast of the print.

1. First, fill your measuring cup with water and put it in the mixing container.

2. Then add two measuring cups full of Plaster of Paris powder to the container.

3. Stir with your stick until all the lumps are gone. The mixture should be as thick as glue paste. If it is too thick, add a little more water. If it is too thin, add a little more powder.

4. Gently pour the mixture into your footprint mould.

5. If you have extra mixture, put it in a sealable bag.

6. The cast will take anywhere from 15 minutes to an hour to **set** or go hard. If the ground (or sand) is wet, it will take longer. While you wait, put all your equipment and rubbish in your backpack.

7. When you think the cast is ready, gently touch the top. If your finger doesn't make a mark, it is set.

8. Hold the plastic ring and lift the cast directly up. Don't worry if there is earth or sand stuck to the bottom at this stage.

9. Put your cast in a plastic bag to take home.

10. Let it dry out completely for a few hours.

11. Cut off the plastic ring and wash the cast under a tap to remove any dirt or sand.

12. If you want, you can paint your cast!

Why is my cast raised up?

Your plaster cast is a negative of the footprint! If you push your cast into a block of playdough and peel it off, the playdough will have a **positive** footprint.

One day, in the 1960s, a farmer in Australia found a rock which looked just like a plaster cast of a footprint. It was the negative imprint of a small dinosaur about the size of a chicken who lived about 95 million years ago! Way back then, the dinosaur had left a footprint, or **imprint**, in the mud, and fine sediment (like sand) filled the imprint in. Over time, the sediment hardened into a layer just like Plaster of Paris. It was covered with other dirt and eventually, it was hidden deep inside a hill.

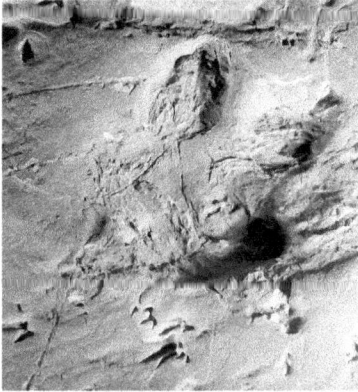

A real dinosaur stampede!

Scientists from the Queensland Museum were excited when they saw the rock the farmer had found. They travelled to the place it was found and carefully dug down until they reached the **sedimentary** layer. Then they dug sideways, following the sandy rock until the sedimentary layer was exposed. Eventually, they found 3,300 dinosaur footprints which told a story of a dinosaur **stampede**! Small dinosaurs had run away from a large predator (with much bigger feet) which was trying to eat them! This special place is called Lark Quarry. It is near a town called Winton. Maybe you can visit one day. Lark Quarry is the only place in the world where a dinosaur stampede has been found... and it all started with one negative footprint!

Experiment 2

Making a camera

Do you remember that cameras have negatives too?

In the story, Wong set camera traps to take photos of animals. When the animals tripped a switch, the shutter of the camera opened, and light travelled through the small **aperture**, burning into the chemicals on small squares of camera film. The more light that entered, the darker the image appeared on the film. So white looked dark, and black looked white. This negative is just like your footprint plaster cast!

The lens in a camera is **convex**, or curved outwards. This captures the light and directs it towards the film. It also makes the image on the film upside down. Once people understood this optical **phenomenon**, it was used to create the first ever photographs!

In a pinhole camera (or a **camera obscura**), light travels through a small opening, **projecting** an image on the opposite surface. Let's make a pinhole camera to see how this works…

(This experiment is best done at night.)

You will need:

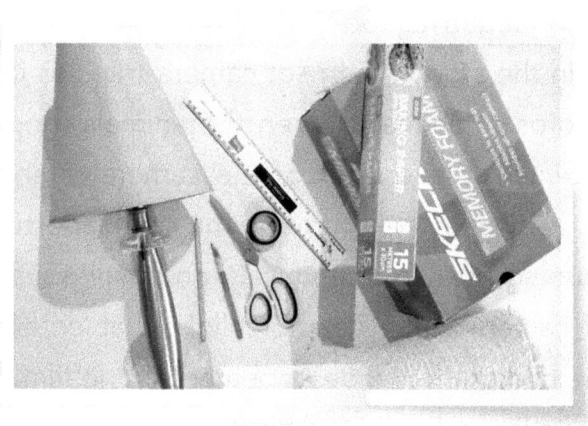

An empty shoebox with a lid

A pencil

Scissors

A craft knife (ask an adult to help with this one…)

A ruler

Sticky tape

A blanket

Wax paper

A lamp without a lamp shade

Steps:

1. Use the ruler to measure the middle of one of the ends of the shoebox then punch a small hole in the middle with the pencil.

2. Measure the middle of the other end of the box and mark it with the pencil. On this end, draw a square which measures 5cm on each side with the pencil mark in the middle. (It doesn't have to be exactly in the middle, but close is good.)

3. Use the craft knife (and an adult) to cut out the square.

4. Use scissors to cut a square of wax paper with each side measuring 8cm.

5. Place the wax paper square over the square hole and tape the edges down.

6. Turn on the lamp and turn off the room lights.

7. Stand away from the lamp holding the box up at arm's length at about eye level. The small hole must face the lamp and the wax paper must face you.

8. Ask a friend to cover your head and half the box with a blanket to make sure it is extra dark.

9. Can you see an upside-down image of the lamp on the wax paper?

You just made a camera!

The first ever cameras used this method!

© CREATIVE COMMONS

Experiment 3

Measuring the tide

A long time ago, the sea water level rose and drowned Sundaland, forming the island we now know as Borneo. Seawater rises and falls every day too, but not as much. This daily rise and fall is called the tide and tides are controlled by the moon. The moon is like a huge magnet which attracts water. All the water in the earth is pulled towards the moon so, if you are on the same side of the earth as the moon, the water will be higher and if you are on the opposite side of the earth from the moon, it will also be higher. The tide is low in between. The moon goes round the earth once every 24 hours which means there are two high tides, and two low tides every 24 hours. You can measure it if you are lucky enough to go to the beach.

You will need:

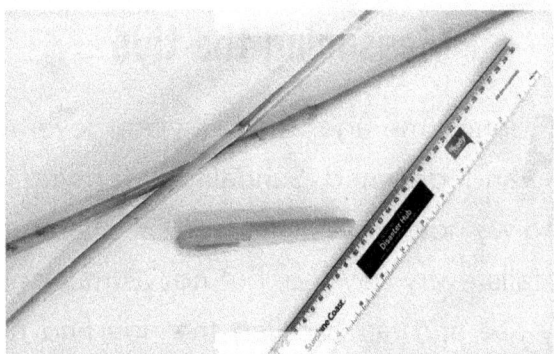

Two straight sticks between 50cm and 1m long
A thick waterproof pen or nail polish
A ruler
Patience!

Steps

Before you leave home

1. Use the ruler and waterproof pen or nail polish to mark centimetre (or inch) lines along one of your sticks starting with zero about 20cm along the stick and going all the way to the end. This stick will measure water rising.

2. Use the ruler and waterproof pen or nail polish to mark centimetre (or inch) lines all the way along the other stick. This stick will measure water falling.

At the beach

1. If you can, find a calm area away from waves.

2. Push the first stick into the sand at the very edge of the water so that the zero is level with the sand.

3. With an adult's permission (or with an adult), wade into the water up to your waist. Stand the second stick up in the

sand next to you and push it down so that the top of the stick is at water level.

4. Now go and build a sandcastle, go for a swim, or play with your dog!

5. When you are ready to leave the beach, check your sticks.

What did you find?

Has the water risen or fallen?

How high has the tide risen or fallen?

Does this mean the tide has come in or out?

New words

Some of the words or phrases in this book are bold. Here's what they mean. They are in alphabetical order. If a word (or phrase) starts with A, AN or THE, it is a noun (a person, place or thing). If it starts with TO BE, it is a verb (a doing word). An adverb describes (or adds to) a verb, and an adjective describes (or adds to) a noun. I reckon it should be called an adnoun!

To abandon — give up doing something.

Adapted — (verb) became adjusted to new conditions.

An amphibian — a cold blooded animal with a backbone that starts life in the water and then lives on land as an adult. For example, frogs and toads are amphibians.

To be anesthetised — given drugs to temporarily go to sleep.

An animal/human conflict — a situation when animals and humans don't get on.

An aperture — an opening.

To be attuned to — having a deep understanding with something (like nature).

A bachelor — a man who is not married, or a male animal without a mate.

A camera obscura — a pinhole camera.

A camera trap — a camera attached to a sensor which takes pictures of animals.

A cartridge — a container which holds something. For instance, film, ink, or gunpowder.

Cautiously — (adverb) doing something carefully to avoid problems.

To be coaxed — gently persuaded or talked into doing something.

A continent — one of seven large land masses on Earth.

To contradict — two things that are in conflict with each other.

Conservationists — (noun) people who act to protect the environment and wildlife.

To be convex — (adjective) having a curved surface which bends outwards.

To be decimated — destroyed.

Decreasing — becoming smaller.

Dense — (adjective) when a substance is compact or close together. For example, a dense fog.

To be developed — treat a film with chemicals to make a photographic print.

Dexterous — (adjective) having skill, especially with your hands.

Dung — (noun) animal poo.

To be eroded — worn away by wind or water.

The evidence — facts or information that support a belief.

Fibres — (noun) threads from a plant.

A frame — a square of photographic film.

Gondwana — an ancient super-continent containing all the land on earth.

To be in the field — in the environment conducting research.

To be increasing — becoming larger.

An imprint — an impress, or stamp, on a surface. For example, a footprint.

Jurassic — (adjective) describes the second period of the Mesozoic era between the Triassic and Cretaceous periods.

A machete — a broad, heavy knife.

A macaque — a type of monkey.

Manure — (noun) another word for animal poo or dung.

A matriarch — a female head of a family or herd.

To be menacing — to look very scary.

To migrate — to move from one region or habitat to another to find food, or because of climate.

To misfire — to fail to go off, or fire. A camera can misfire. So can a gun.

Musth — (noun or adjective) a condition when an animal is aggressive and unpredictable.

A negative — the image made of photographic film before a print is made.

To observe — to watch.

A pachyderm — a large animal with thick skin. Elephants, rhinos and hippos are pachyderms.

To penetrate — go into or through something.

To persist — continue even though it is difficult.

A phenomenon — a fact which can be observed.

To pivot — turn around quickly on the spot.

A positive — a photographic print made from a negative.

Projecting — (verb) making light or shadow to fall on a surface. For instance, you could project a movie onto a screen.

Pygmy — something very small.

To be roaming — moving around over a large area.

To saunter — walk slowly. To stroll.

Sedimentary — (adjective) describes a layer of rock deposited by water or air.

To sense — be aware of or detect something.

A sensor — a device that detects something.

To set — harden from a liquid into a solid.

Shards — (noun) broken pieces, usually with sharp edges.

To be shielded — protected from danger.

To be solitary — alone.

A stampede — a rush of panicking animals.

Stealth — (noun) cautious action or movement.

Sundaland — land mass in South-eastern Asia when sea levels were lower.

A technician — a person who works with technical equipment, like photo developing equipment.

To be unique — one of a kind.

A wildlife corridor — a narrow area of wildlife habitat linking two larger natural areas together.

Do you want to help rainforest animals?

"Can you help me?"

Here are a few ideas:

- Lend this book to your friends so they can learn about pygmy elephants too
- Do a school project on pygmy elephants

- Adopt a sun bear with your family or your class at www.bsbcc.my
- Join the Wildlife Wong Kids' Club and download your free Nature Journal at www.sarahrpye.com
- If you waste less and buy less, less rainforest needs to be cut down and elephants will still have their home
- Volunteer with a conservation group in your own area – the entire environment needs help, not just Borneo!
- If you are old enough, connect with me on Facebook or Instagram
- Email me your review of this book. If it is written well, I might ask you to write one for the next book, and you will get your picture in the front!

For teachers and parents:

Sarah Pye is available for speaking engagements, keynote addresses and hands-on workshops online and in person. For more information visit:

⊕ **www.sarahrpye.com**

This book was printed on demand (POD) which reduces waste and saves our trees.